WHALES

Jen Green

GROLIER

an imprint of

SCHOLASTIC

www.scholastic.com/librarypublishing

Published 2008 by Grolier
An imprint of Scholastic Library Publishing
Old Sherman Turnpike, Danbury,
Connecticut 06816

For The Brown Reference Group plc
Project Editor: Jolyon Goddard
Copy-editors: Lesley Ellis, Lisa Hughes,
    Wendy Horobin
Picture Researcher: Clare Newman
Designers: Jeni Child, Lynne Ross,
    Sarah Williams
Managing Editor: Bridget Giles

Volume ISBN-13: 978-0-7172-6264-9
Volume ISBN-10: 0-7172-6264-2

**Library of Congress
Cataloging-in-Publication Data**

Nature's children. Set 2.
    p. cm.
  Includes bibliographical references and
index.
  ISBN-13: 978-0-7172-8081-0
  ISBN-10: 0-7172-8081-0
  1. Animals--Encyclopedias, Juvenile. I.
Grolier (Firm)
  QL49.N383 2007
  590--dc22

2007026928

Printed and bound in China

PICTURE CREDITS

Front Cover: **Nature PL**: Brandon Cole.

Back Cover: **Nature PL**: Brandon Cole,
Doug Perrine, Doc White; **Shutterstock**:
Brett Atkins.

FLPA: Flip Nicklin/Minden Pictures 20, 30,
38, 42; **Nature PL**: Doug Allan 34, Brandon
Cole 2–3, 12, 45, Martha Holmes 23, Todd
Pusser 19; **NHPA**: A.N.T. Photolibrary 37;
Photolibrary.com: Gerard Soury 11, 41;
Shutterstock: Brett Atkins 29, Richard
Fitzer 15, Fernando Rodrigues 33; **Still
Pictures**: BIOS/Yves Lefevre 8, Adrian
Dorst 5, Harpe/Wildlife 7, H. Schmidbauer
4, 26–27, 46, Douglas Seifert/UNEP 16.

Contents

FACT FILE: Whales

Class	Mammals (Mammalia)
Order	Toothed whales and baleen whales (Cetacea)
Families	14 families
Genera	41 genera
Species	About 86 species, including about 46 species of dolphins and porpoises
World distribution	Varies with species
Habitat	Both coastal waters and the open ocean; river dolphins live in certain rivers
Distinctive physical characteristics	Torpedo-shaped body with flippers and twin tail flukes; one or two blowholes on top of the head; some whales grow to an enormous size
Habits	Many whales live in groups; some whales migrate very long distances
Diet	Toothed whales eat fish, squid, and marine mammals; baleen whales eat plankton and small fish

Introduction

The blue whale is the biggest animal in the world. Not all whales are large, though. The whale family includes dolphins and porpoises, some of which are about the size of humans.

Size is one of the most remarkable features of whales. But they are amazing in other ways, too. Whales are very clever. Most whales live in groups, called pods, and take good care of one another. Whales can also sing. Like most whales, orcas, or killer whales, live in pods. Each pod has its own unique dialect of sounds. Orcas can easily recognize their own pod from several miles away based on the difference in calls. Pods with similar dialects sometimes form even bigger groups, or clans.

An orca rises out of the sea.

Sea Mammals

A whale has a similar shape to a fish, with a finned tail and torpedo-shaped body. But whales are not fish. They are mammals, like dogs, cats, horses, monkeys, and humans. Whales are marine mammals—they live in the sea.

All mammals share certain features. They are all warm-blooded, which means their body stays the same temperature no matter how cold or hot the outside temperature is. All mammals have some hair on their body, although whales are not very hairy. In many whales, the hair consists of a few whiskers. Some whales only have hair as babies.

Like all mammals, whales breathe air, even though they swim in the sea. They also give birth to live young, instead of laying eggs. Young whales drink their mother's milk, just like humans and other mammals do when young.

A young southern right whale, or calf, swims alongside its mother.

A humpback whale
shows a flipper. Whales
use their flippers for
steering underwater.

Living in Water

Whales are found throughout the oceans. Some whales swim mainly in shallow coastal waters, whereas others swim in the open ocean. River dolphins spend their life in freshwater rivers. Many types of whales swim huge distances through the oceans as they move between their feeding and breeding grounds. These journeys are called **migrations**.

Believe it or not, whales were once land animals. Experts believe whales are descended from four-legged mammals that lived on land more than 70 million years ago. They gradually took to the water, perhaps to find food when food on land became scarce. Over many generations, the whales gradually became more suited to their watery habitat, through a process called **evolution**. Small changes occurred over thousands of years. For example, whales now have flippers instead of the hands or paws that their ancestors had. However, the bones inside a whale's flipper are very similar to the bones in a human's hand.

The Scale of Whales

The scientific name of the whale family is cetaceans (SI-TAY-SHUNS). That comes from the Greek word for "sea-monster." Since ancient times, people have been awed by the huge scale of whales. The blue whale is the largest animal that has ever lived on Earth—bigger than any dinosaur that ever existed. An adult blue whale can grow to 90 feet (27.5 m) long and weigh 148 tons (150 metric tons). That's more than 20 African elephants! Its heart alone is the size of a small automobile. The main blood vessel from the blue whale's heart, the aorta, is large enough for a person to crawl inside.

At the other end of the scale, dolphins and porpoises are the smallest whales. Hector's dolphin and the vaquita are just 4 to 5 feet (1.2–1.5 m) long and weigh 90 to 110 pounds (40–50 kg).

The land-living ancestors of whales were much smaller than the whales of today. Whales have been able to grow so big because their great weight is supported by water.

The biggest whale, the blue whale, was almost hunted to extinction in the first half of the 20th century. Protected since 1966, its numbers are increasing.

A humpback whale opens its mouth and reveals its baleen plates.

Meet the Family

There are more than 80 **species**, or types, of whales. Experts divide the whale family into two main groups: **baleen** whales and toothed whales. The two groups eat different foods and catch their food in different ways.

Baleen whales are named for the long plates of a horny substance, called baleen, that hang down inside their mouth. They use these plates to filter food from the water. Baleen whales include the blue whale, the humpback, fin, and gray whale.

In general, the largest whales are baleen whales. However, the group of toothed whales includes the mighty sperm whale, which grows to 65 feet (20 m) long. Toothed whales also include dolphins, porpoises, the beluga, and the orca, or killer whale. Male toothed whales are larger than the females. Female baleen whales, however, are generally larger than the males. So the largest blue whale that has ever swam in the oceans was most likely female.

Built to Swim

Whales spend their whole life in water. It's therefore not surprising that they are superb swimmers. Their sleek, tapering shape slides easily through water. Unlike a fish's tail, which points up and down, a whale's tail points side to side, parallel to the surface of the water. A whale swims forward by beating its powerful tail up and down. A whale's tail is made of solid muscle not bone. The tail ends in twin fins called **flukes**.

Most whales have a dorsal, or back, fin that helps them maneuver. Whales also use their front limbs, called flippers, for steering and turning. Humpback whales have particularly long flippers—and tail flukes. From tip to tip, a humpback's flukes can grow to one-third of the whale's body length. So a 50-foot (16-m) humpback might have flukes that are almost 17 feet (5 m) across.

The humpback whale
has a massive tail.

Sperm whales have
the largest brain of any
living or extinct animal.

Deep Divers

Whales are skilled divers. Toothed whales make very deep dives to catch their food. The sperm whale is the champion diver. It descends to the dark depths 3,000 feet (1,000 m) below to catch its favorite food, giant squid. Baleen whales usually only dive to about 500 feet (150 m). That's because their food floats or swims near the surface of the sea.

A whale prepares to dive by taking a deep breath. On a long dive, its heart rate slows, which makes the oxygen in its lungs last longer. Also on long dives, the whale's blood travels only to important parts of the body, such as the brain, heart, and lungs.

The whale's blood carries more oxygen than the blood of land animals such as humans. No human can hold his or her breath for more than a couple of minutes. But sperm whales can stay underwater for up to an amazing 90 minutes.

Coming Up for Air

Whales cannot extract oxygen from the water, like fish do with their **gills**. Sooner or later, they have to surface to breathe. Whales don't breathe through their mouth, but through the **blowhole** on top of their head. The blowhole is the whale's nostrils. Baleen whales have two blowholes—similar to a person's two nostrils—whereas toothed whales have just one. The position on top of the head allows the whale to breathe without having to lift its head out of the water.

The stale air is breathed out first. The loud whooshing sound of a whale exhaling can be heard a long way away! The whale then fills its lungs with fresh air. The blowhole shuts as the whale dives, and water closes over it again.

A whale would drown if it did not surface for air every now and then. Because a whale must return to the surface regularly for air, it is unable to sleep for hours at a time. Instead, it takes a series of short naps throughout the day.

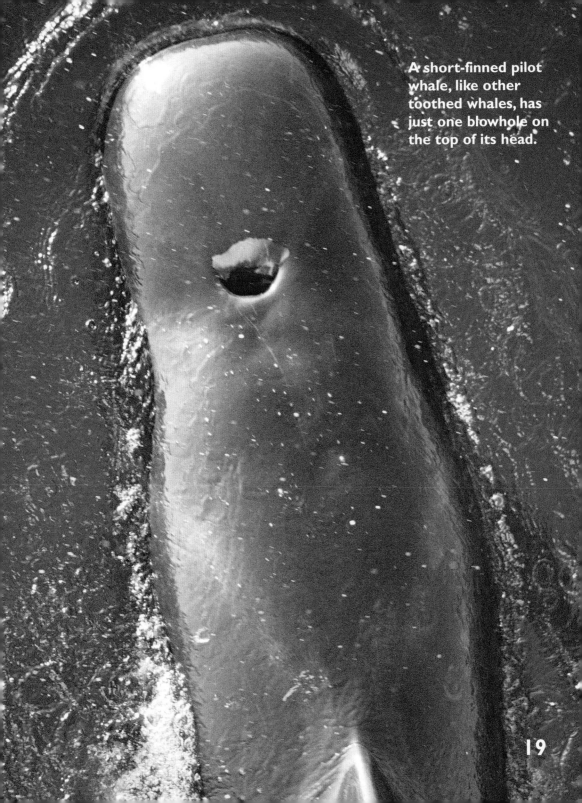

A short-finned pilot whale, like other toothed whales, has just one blowhole on the top of its head.

19

A blue whale's spout is a tall column, as high as 30 feet (9 m).

Spouting Off

When a whale surfaces, the first thing it does is breathe out through its blowhole. The tall spout can be seen from quite a distance. It looks like a fountain of water, but in fact, it is a jet of air containing water vapor. The moisture in the spout becomes visible as it cools, turning into tiny water droplets in the air. When you exhale on a cool day, you can see your breath do the same thing.

Different species of whales produce spouts of various shapes. The gray whale has a low, wide spout. The sperm whale's spout shoots out at an angle. The blue whale has a tall, thin spout, whereas the right whale's spout is heart-shaped. Experts can identify the type of whale from the shape of the spout.

Useful Blubber

Whales can keep warm even in icy waters with the help of a thick layer of fat just below their skin. This layer is called **blubber**. Whales that live in cold polar seas have extra-thick blubber. The bowhead whale of Arctic waters has blubber up to 2 feet (0.6 m) thick! The blubber keeps it snug, like a thick fleecy coat.

The whale's blubber also acts as an energy store—like a built-in pantry. When the whale visits parts of the oceans where food is plentiful, it eats a huge amount, puts on weight, and stores the extra fat as blubber. When food is scarce, the whale lives off the stored fat, which provides the energy that the whale needs to keep going.

Bowhead whales spend their whole life swimming in cold Arctic seas.

Color and Disguise

Whales vary in color. Small toothed whales called belugas are snowy white. Pilot whales are jet black. Orcas have very distinct black-and-white coloration. But most whales are shades of gray or brown.

Many whales are dark on top with a pale belly, or underside. This pattern is called **countershading**. It helps to conceal the whale from other animals, either above or below. Birds looking down from the sky would find it hard to spot the whale's dark back against the dark ocean. Fish or other prey looking up from below have difficulty spotting the pale belly against the sunlit surface of the sea.

Underwater Senses

If you have ever opened your eyes underwater, things probably looked blurry. Luckily for whales, their eyes are suited to seeing underwater. However, even whales cannot see very far in dark or murky water. While they can focus well in water, they cannot see well in air like humans can.

Whales have no sense of smell. But they do have a keen sense of taste. Hearing is thought to be the whale's most important and most utilized sense. They can detect very high- and low-pitched sounds out of the range of human hearing. Sound travels long distances very quickly in water. That helps whales to find out what's going on a long way away in very little time.

With its distinctive black-and-white coloration, this somersaulting orca is easy to identify.

Baleen Whales

Baleen whales feed on small fish, shrimp, and even tinier, floating living things called **plankton**. They filter their food out of the water using the horny baleen plates that hang down from their upper jaw. The plates act like a giant comb.

How exactly does a baleen whale get its food? The whale feeds by swimming along in food-rich seas with its mouth open. Tons of water containing tiny creatures gush into the huge mouth. Water spills out again through the baleen, but the small creatures are trapped inside. The whale collects the food on its giant tongue and then swallows.

Baleen whales are also called great whales because of their size. So how do they get so big by eating only tiny creatures? Well, they have to eat huge amounts. A blue whale swallows up to 9,000 pounds (4,000 kg) of plankton in a single day.

The humpback is a type of baleen whale. It feeds on small fish and shrimplike animals called krill.

A pod of male narwhals swims off the coast of Baffin Island, Canada. A narwhal's tusk can grow to 10 feet (3 m) long.

Toothed Whales

Toothed whales eat larger prey than baleen whales—mostly fish and squid. They use their teeth only to seize their slippery prey, not to chew them up. The whale swallows its food without chewing. Some toothed whales scoop their prey off the seabed using suction, much like a vacuum cleaner!

Most toothed whales, including dolphins and orcas, live in groups called pods or schools. Some of these pods contain hundreds of whales. The whales work together to surround and trap schools of fish.

Toothed whales include the amazing narwhal, which swims in Arctic waters. The male narwhal has just one long tooth, that grows out from his jaw to form a long, spiralling tusk. Some people think that a narwhal's tusk, washed up on the seashore, might have given rise to the legend of the unicorn.

Hunting with Sound

Toothed whales, such as dolphins and orcas, hunt by using sound in a special way. They produce streams of clicking sounds. The sound waves spread out through the water. When they hit an object, such as a fish, they bounce back. The whale listens to the echoes carefully because they allow it to pinpoint its prey. The time taken for the sounds to bounce back gives the whale not only information about the fish's size and shape, but also tells the whale the direction in which the fish is traveling.

This amazing technique is called **echolocation**. On land, bats use a very similar method to prey on insects. When hunting in a group, whales also use sound to coordinate the hunt. They squeak and whistle to one another. That way each animal knows exactly where the others are as they close in on their prey.

Toothed whales such as this beluga, or white whale, use echolocation to catch their prey.

A pod of belugas migrates through sea ice off the coast of Canada.

Long Journeys

Some whales travel thousands of miles each year on their migrations. In spring, many of the great whales swim to cold polar waters to feast on plankton. In fall they swim all the way back to breed in warm, tropical seas. During these long journeys they usually swim day and night, without stopping to rest or even feed.

The gray whale makes the longest migration of any mammal in the sea or on land. It spends each summer off the coast of Alaska. Then it swims south, all the way down the coast of North America, to the warm waters off Mexico. It covers about 125 miles (200 km) a day on a trip that might take three months. Each year, it completes a round trip of up to 12,500 miles (20,000 km)!

Group Living

A few whales are solitary, meaning they live alone, but most whales spend their life in a group. Members of the pod talk to one another in squeaks, moans, roars, and rumbles. They can also communicate by touching one another with their body and flippers.

Scientists believe whales also send signals by leaping out of the water and splashing down again. That is called **breaching**. Whales also smack the surface of the water with their tail, making a big splash. That is called lobtailing.

If one whale in a pod is hurt or upset, the others crowd around and comfort it. There are many stories of whales coming to the rescue of others, particularly baby whales, or **calves**. In one account, several people saw two grown-up whales rescue a calf that was stranded on a ridge of sand in coastal waters. The adults wriggled up onto the ridge and sandwiched the calf between them. Then all three slid off into the water. Mission accomplished!

A humpback whale and a calf breach together.

In the breeding season, male narwhals fight over a female, or cow, using their long tusk as a weapon.

38

Pairing Up

Whales are ready to breed for the first time at about six years old. After that, females usually give birth every two or three years. **Bulls**, or adult males, and **cows**, or adult females, get to know one another by playing—nuzzling and splashing in the water. They "sing" to one another as their huge bodies touch. Male humpbacks court the females by singing long, complicated songs made of snores, groans, roars, clicks, and squeals. The bull sings for hours with his head hanging low. The songs of the male humpback are among the loudest, longest songs in nature.

If two bulls want to **mate** with the same cow, they may fight. Narwhals are said to spar using their long tusk. Once partners have been chosen, the pair is very affectionate. They roll in the water and stroke each other with their flippers. Some types of whales stay together for life.

A Calf Is Born

Whale calves take even longer to develop inside their mother than human babies. It takes 10 to 12 months before the young whale is ready to be born.

Young whales are not born with thick blubber like the adults. So it's best they are born in warm, sheltered waters. That's why some whales migrate all the way to the tropics to give birth. Whales that remain in cold seas, such as bowhead whales and narwhals, usually move to calm, shallow waters to breed.

Some baby whales are huge. A newborn blue whale is as long as a grown-up elephant and weighs about 2½ tons (2.5 metric tons)!

A southern right whale mother swims alongside her calf.

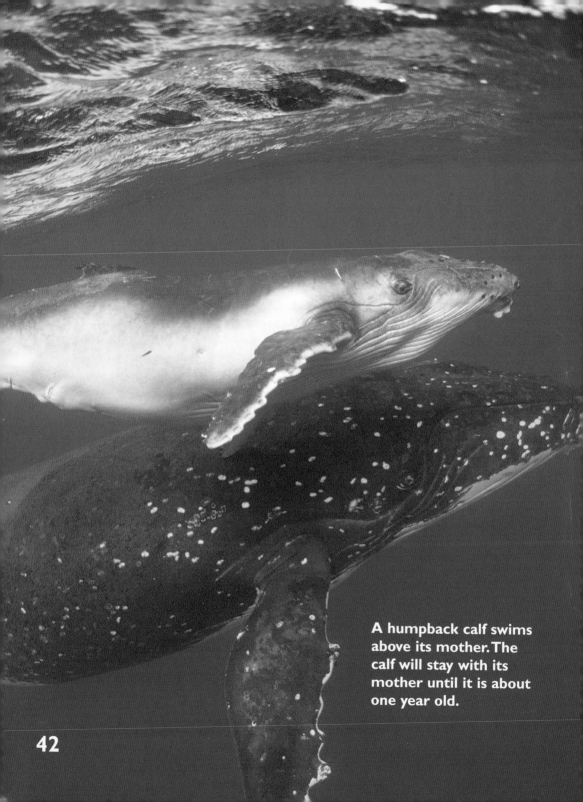

A humpback calf swims above its mother. The calf will stay with its mother until it is about one year old.

First Things First

Mother whales usually give birth to just one
baby, though occasionally twins are born. Most
calves come out tail-first. The baby is born
underwater. But it needs to breathe almost
immediately. The mother gently nudges it
to the surface with her snout. In species such
as dolphins, another experienced female acts
as midwife, helping with the birth.

One of the first things a young whale learns
is to come up for air. It learns that by watching
and copying its mother. The large mother and
her small calf dive, surface, and breathe together,
like a synchronized swimming team. Once the
calf has learned this lesson it will be ready for the
rougher waters of the open ocean.

Hungry Eaters

A whale calf is born hungry! Like all mammals, it drinks its mother's milk at first. A baby blue whale needs to guzzle what would amount to a whole bathful of milk every day! The mother's milk contains all the nourishment the baby needs and is high in fat, so the calf grows quickly.

Unlike human babies, who are helpless at first, the whale calf is strong and well-prepared for life in the ocean. Even so, baleen calves continue to **nurse** from their mothers for six to eight months. Toothed whales nurse for up to two years, before graduating to a diet of fish and squid. The reason toothed calves nurse for so much longer is that it takes them a while to get the hang of the hunting skills they will need to catch their own food.

A pod of sperm whales swims in warm waters near the Azores in the Atlantic Ocean.

If an orca survives
into adulthood, it
will probably live
to at least 50 years.

First Journey

Many whales remain in the warm breeding waters until spring. Then it's time to start the long journey to feeding grounds in colder seas. The mothers and calves are the last to leave. That gives the babies as much time as possible to get their strength up for the long, grueling migration ahead.

The calf swims by its mother's side throughout the long journey. The females are very protective, and will do anything to save their calf from predators such as sharks and orcas. Finally, the journey ends at the feeding grounds. There, the whales feast for days on end.

Young toothed whales stick close to their mother until she prepares to give birth again. Then, the calf is on its own, though it still swims with the pod. With luck, it will live for many years—up to 80 or more years for some whale species—and have many youngsters of its own.

Whale Watching

People used to hunt whales for their meat and blubber. So many whales were killed that many species, that were once plentiful, became scarce. Now as a result of an international ban, only a few countries, including Canada, Iceland, and Norway, practice whale hunting, or whaling. Instead of hunting whales, people enjoy learning about these beautiful animals and watching them in the wild.

People flock to coasts to see whales swim by on migration. Some whale-watchers travel out to meet the whales in small boats. The huge beasts are quite gentle. Some people get close enough to touch them. Whale watching is an amazing experience, so try it if you get the chance!

In recent years, scientists have made many new discoveries about whales, but there's still a lot they don't know. The more we learn, the more we appreciate these clever animals and their gentle mastery of the watery world.

Words to Know

Baleen The long, horny plates that hang down from the upper jaw of some whales. The plates let the whale filter out plankton and small creatures from the sea for food.

Blowhole The opening on top of a whale's head that acts as a nostril.

Blubber A layer of fat beneath the whale's skin that keeps it warm in water.

Breaching Leaping out of the water.

Bulls Male whales.

Calves Young whales.

Counter-shading When an animal is dark on top with a pale underside.

Cows Female whales.

Echolocation   A technique used by some toothed whales to find their way and locate food underwater.

Evolution   The process of gradual change in animal species that makes them better suited to their surroundings.

Flukes   A whale's tail fins.

Gills   The feathery structures in a fish's head that allow it to breathe underwater.

Mate   To come together to produce young.

Migrations   Long, regular journeys, often between an animal's feeding and breeding grounds.

Nurse   To drink milk from a mother's body.

Plankton   Small animals and algae that float in the oceans.

Species   The scientific word for animals of the same type that breed together.

Find Out More

Books

DK Publishing. *Whale*. Eyewitness Books. New York, New York: DK Publishing, Inc., 2004.

Leon, V. *A Pod of Killer Whales: The Mysterious Life of the Intelligent Orca*. Jean-Michel Cousteau Presents. Montrose, California: London Town Press, 2006.

Web sites

Creature Feature: Orcas
www.nationalgeographic.com/kids/creature_feature/ 0105/orcas.html
Facts and footage of orcas, or killer whales.

What Is a Whale?
www.enchantedlearning.com/subjects/whales/allabout/
A ton of information about whales.

Index